Sekiya Miyoshi

JONAH
AND THE
BIG FISH

Abingdon Press/Nashville

A long time ago there lived a giant fish who glowed as if he had all the colors
of the rainbow.
He came up out of the ocean one day and saw a young man sleeping
on top of the cliffs.

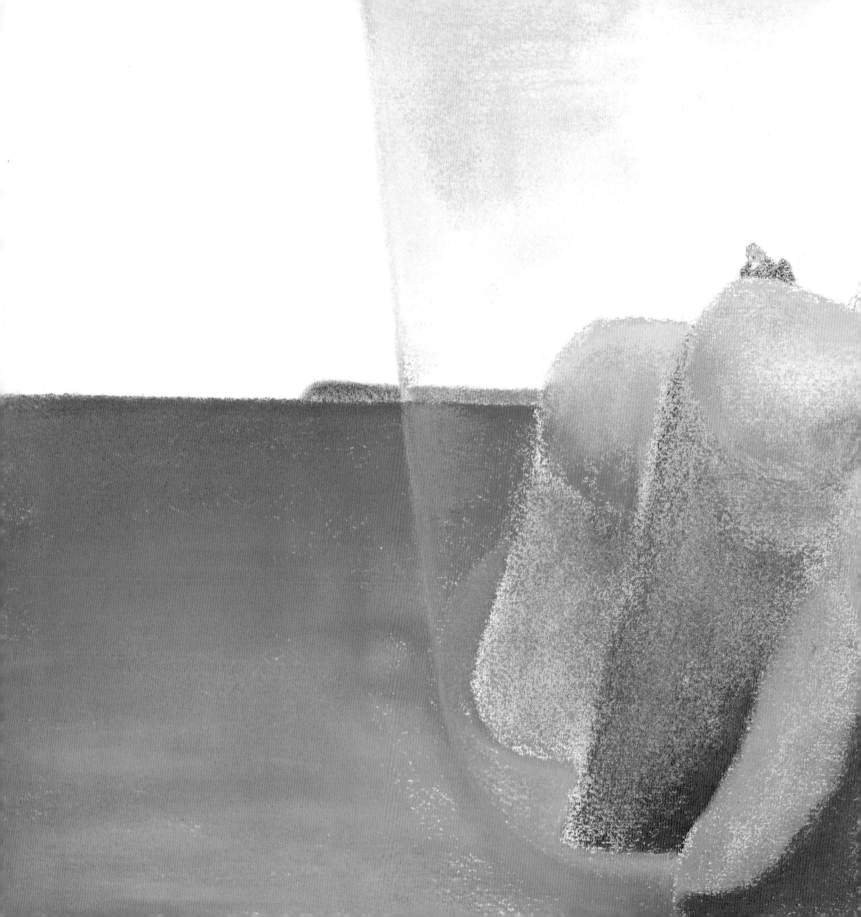

A voice spoke to the young man in his sleep:
"Jonah, get up and go to Nineveh, the capitol of Assyria.
Go and tell the people that I shall destroy their city
for all the bad things they have done."
Jonah awoke and looked about him, but he did not know
where the voice came from.

Jonah thought: "God has spoken to me. But why to me? Nineveh is so far away from here. The people there are bad, but what does it have to do with me? Why should I have to go to Nineveh?"

Jonah did not want to go to Nineveh. But he was afraid of what might happen if he did not go. Secretly he left his house, his land, and his donkey and fled from God.

He walked a long time before he came to the seaport Joppa.
There Jonah boarded a ship where he hoped God would not find him.

The ship Jonah took was to sail to Tarshish, at the end of the sea.
The sky was blue and the water calm.
Jonah felt safe aboard the ship. He became tired and fell asleep.

The big fish followed Jonah all the time.

Suddenly there was a strong wind. The ship was tossed to and fro.
The storm drove the ship away from the coast, far out into the raging sea.

The captain and the sailors prayed to their gods, "Save us! Save us!" But the storm grew stronger. Jonah awoke and knew what was happening.
When the captain of the ship asked,
"Where is this storm coming from? Who is responsible for the storm?"
Jonah answered, "I am guilty. I wanted to hide from God.
Toss me into the sea, and it
will be calm again."

So the sailors tossed Jonah into the wild sea. And the ocean became calm.

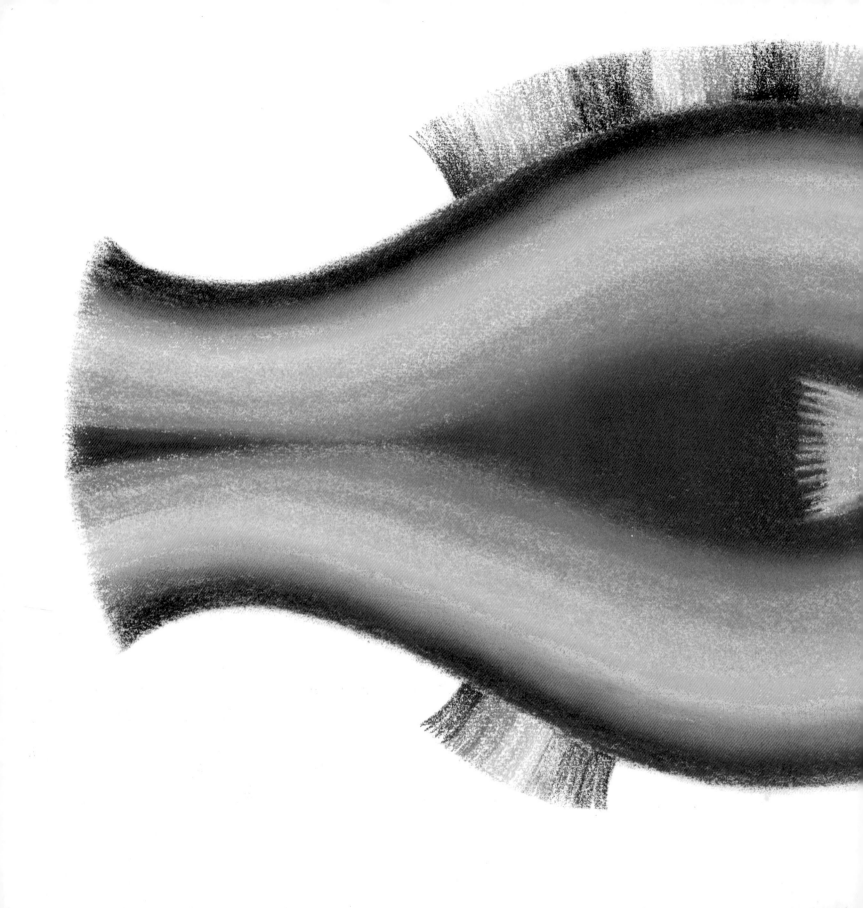

The big fish was waiting in the water with its mouth wide open.
With one gulp Jonah was swallowed.

Now the big fish swam around with Jonah in its belly.
In the darkness of the belly Jonah prayed fearfully to God.

After three days and nights the big fish's mouth opened.
Jonah was flung into the air and landed on the beach.
He breathed the fresh air deeply and enjoyed the warm sunshine.
Then again he heard the voice, "Jonah, get up and go to Nineveh."

What a miracle! He had landed close to the city of Nineveh!

This time Jonah obeyed. He went to the gate of Nineveh
and called with a loud voice,
"God will destroy your city in forty days because you are doing evil things!"

Then he quickly ran off and climbed to the top of a hill.
He had a great fear that the people of Nineveh would pursue him.
But the people of Nineveh who had heard Jonah became fearful.
They repented their evil doings and prayed day by day to God,
asking for forgiveness.

From the top of the hill Jonah looked across to the city of Nineveh.
In the burning sun he watched patiently and waited for its destruction.
But nothing happened. The city stayed unharmed.

God had forgiven the people of Nineveh.

Jonah was confused. God doesn't break his promises!
He could not understand it.

While he sat thinking a tall bush started to grow behind him.
Jonah was grateful for the shade it provided.
It turned cool in the evening after the heat of the day.

But at dawn a worm ate all the leaves from the bush.
When the sun rose, Jonah again was standing in the burning heat.
He became sad and angry.
God had sent him to Nineveh to announce the destruction, but the city
remained unharmed. Yesterday the bush grew, in whose shade he sat,
and today it was without leaves, and the sun burned him again.
Jonah was full of anger.

Then Jonah heard God's voice for the third time.
"Why are you angry, Jonah? You feel sorry for the bush,
and you did not even plant it yourself,
and should I not feel sorry for the people of the big city of Nineveh,
whom I have created myself?
They have asked for forgiveness, and I have forgiven them."

Then Jonah knew God's grace and was no longer angry.

Jonah returned to his house, his land, and his donkey.
He worked every day, got married, and lived happily with his wife
and their children. They knew, that God's grace included them too.

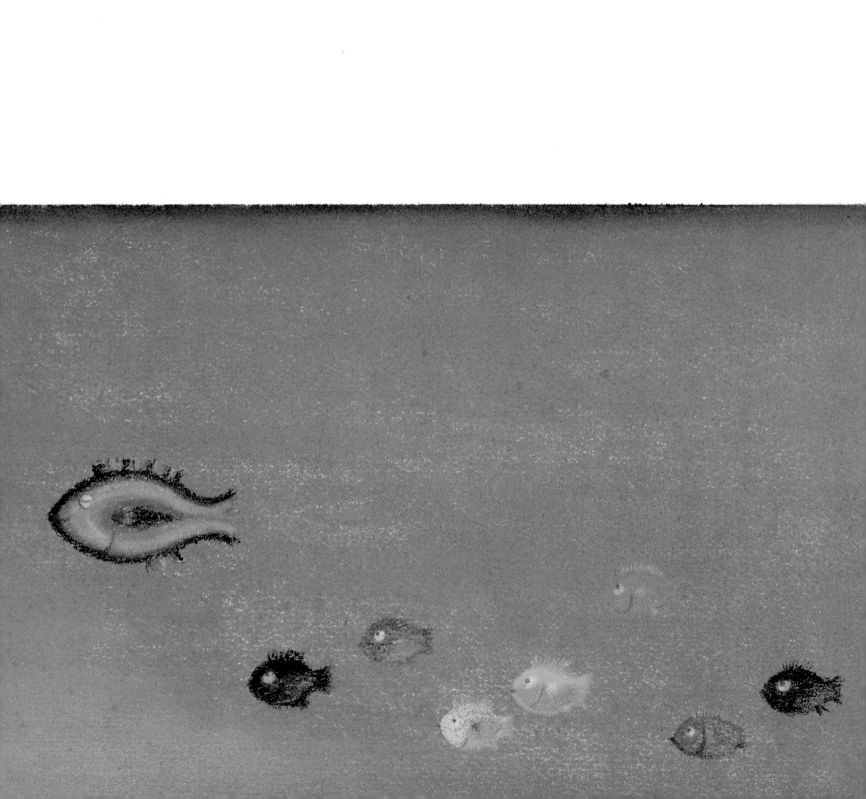

And the great fish had many children and grand-children. And they all glowed
with the colors of the rainbow.
The fish reminds us today of Jonah and his useless flight from God,
of his anger for the people of Nineveh, and how Jonah discovered
that God's grace is greater than his scorn.

JONAH AND THE BIG FISH

English text copyright © 1982 by Abingdon
All rights reserved
Original pictures by Sekiya Miyoshi
© 1977 by Shiko-Sha Co., Ltd.
All rights reserved
Printed in Japan

ISBN 0-687-20541-7